W9-BSC-343

Marine Biome

by Grace Hansen

Abdo
BIOMES
Kids

abdopublishing.com

Published by Abdo Kids, a division of ABDO, PO Box 398166, Minneapolis, Minnesota 55439.

Copyright © 2017 by Abdo Consulting Group, Inc. International copyrights reserved in all countries. No part of this book may be reproduced in any form without written permission from the publisher.

Printed in the United States of America, North Mankato, Minnesota.

052016

092016

THIS BOOK CONTAINS
RECYCLED MATERIALS

Photo Credits: iStock, Shutterstock

Production Contributors: Teddy Borth, Jennie Forsberg, Grace Hansen

Design Contributors: Laura Mitchell, Dorothy Toth

Cataloging-in-Publication Data

Names: Hansen, Grace, author.

Title: Marine biome / by Grace Hansen.

Description: Minneapolis, MN : Abdo Kids, [2017] | Series: Biomes |
    Includes bibliographical references and index.

Identifiers: LCCN 2015959117 | ISBN 9781680805048 (lib. bdg.) |
    ISBN 9781680805604 (ebook) | ISBN 9781680806168 (Read-to-me ebook)

Subjects: LCSH: Marine ecology--Juvenile literature.

Classification: DDC 577.7--dc23

LC record available at http://lccn.loc.gov/2015959117

Table of Contents

What is a Biome?

A biome is a large area. It

has certain plants and animals.

It also has a certain climate.

desert

forest

4

freshwater

marine

grassland

tundra

5

Marine Biomes

Marine waters are biomes. There are three main marine biomes. Oceans are the largest biome. They cover most of Earth.

7

Oceans are big bodies of water. The water is very salty. Water is warmer near the **equator**. Water further from the equator is colder.

9

Coral reefs are found in warm waters. The waters are also shallow. Coral reefs need lots of sunlight.

Estuaries are very unique.
They are areas where
freshwater meets ocean.
They are safe places for
fish to have babies.

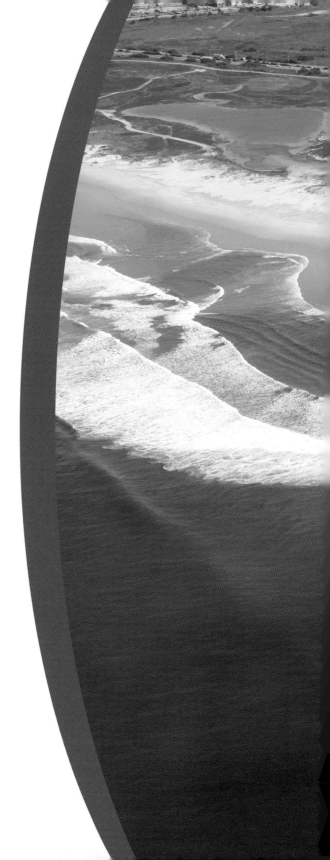

13

Plants

Kelp is an important ocean plant. It is a type of algae. It is food and shelter for many animals. Kelp also makes oxygen!

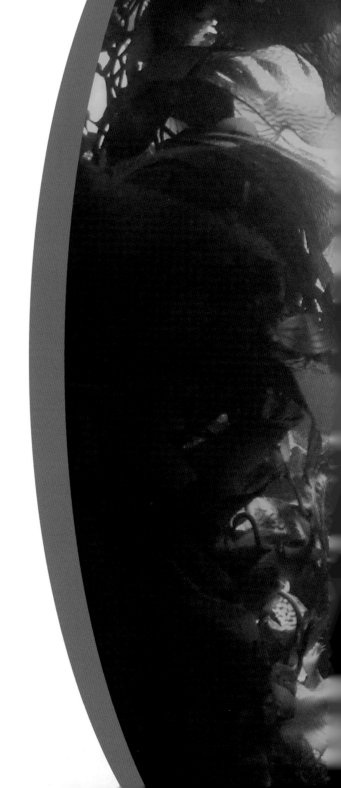

Animals

Corals are not plants. They are animals! Corals attach to reef. They live there forever. They are homes for many other animals.

17

Whales are ocean **mammals**.
They have **blubber**. Blubber
keeps them warm.

Many **crustaceans** live in ocean biomes. They have hard bodies or shells. Hermit crabs live in all marine biomes.

Things You Might See in a Marine Biome

coral reef	estuary	ocean

sea grass

pickleweed

red seaweed

sea anemone

great blue heron

bottlenose dolphin

22

Glossary

algae – small plants that grow in or near water and do not have ordinary leaves, stems, or roots.

blubber – the fat of whales and other large marine mammals.

climate – weather conditions that are usual in an area over a long period of time.

crustacean – a type of animal that has several pairs of legs and a body made up of sections that are covered in a hard outer shell.

equator – imaginary line drawn around the Earth that divides it into the northern and southern hemispheres.

mammal – an animal that feeds milk to its young and usually has hair or fur covering most of its skin.

Index

abdokids.com

Use this code to log on to abdokids.com and access crafts, games, videos, and more!

Abdo Kids Code:
BMK5048